First World War
and Army of Occupation
War Diary
France, Belgium and Germany

16 DIVISION
Divisional Troops
182 Brigade Royal Field Artillery
10 February 1916 - 31 July 1916

WO95/1963/2

The Naval & Military Press Ltd
www.nmarchive.com
Published in association with The National Archives

Published by

The Naval & Military Press Ltd

Unit 10 Ridgewood Industrial Park,

Uckfield, East Sussex,

TN22 5QE England

Tel: +44 (0) 1825 749494

www.naval-military-press.com

www.nmarchive.com

This diary has been reprinted in facsimile from the original. Any imperfections are inevitably reproduced and the quality may fall short of modern type and cartographic standards.

© **Crown Copyright**
Images reproduced by permission of The National Archives, London, England, 2015.

Contents

Document type	Place/Title	Date From	Date To
Heading	WO95/1963/2		
Heading	16th Division 182nd Brigade R.F.A. Feb 1916-Jly 1916 Broken UP		
Heading	War Diary of 182 Brigade R.F.A. From 10.2.16 to 29.2.16		
War Diary	Bordon	10/02/1916	18/02/1916
War Diary	Havre	19/02/1916	21/02/1916
War Diary	Mitterness	22/02/1916	29/02/1916
War Diary	Mazinghem	01/03/1916	07/03/1916
War Diary	Bellery	08/03/1916	07/04/1916
War Diary	Estree Bellery	08/04/1916	09/04/1916
War Diary	Bellery	10/04/1916	16/04/1916
War Diary	Vermelles	17/04/1916	30/04/1916
Heading	Confidential War Diary of 182nd Bde R.F.A. From 1st May 1916 To 31st May 1916		
War Diary	Vermelles	01/05/1916	17/05/1916
War Diary	Loos	18/05/1916	30/05/1916
Heading	Confidential War Diary of 182nd Bde R.F.A. From 1st June To 30th June 1916		
War Diary	Loos Salient	01/06/1916	30/06/1916
Heading	War Diary 182nd Brigade Royal Field Artillery 1st. July to 31st. July 1916 volume no. 6		
War Diary	Loos Salient	01/07/1916	23/07/1916
War Diary	Hulluch Sector	24/07/1916	31/07/1916

WO 45/1963/2

16TH DIVISION

182ND BRIGADE R.F.A.
FEB 1916 - JLY 1916

BROKEN UP

War diary
of
182 Brigade R.F.A.

From 10.2.16. 29.2.16

A.P. Monkton
O in c 182 Bde R.F.A

1.3.16

B.E.F 19.2.16

Army Form C. 2118

WAR DIARY
or
INTELLIGENCE SUMMARY
(Erase heading not required.)

Instructions regarding War Diaries and Intelligence Summaries are contained in F. S. Regs., Part II. and the Staff Manual respectively. Title Pages will be prepared in manuscript.

Place	Date	Hour	Summary of Events and Information	Remarks and references to Appendices
BORDON	10/2/16	6 a.m.	Received order to mobilize on form the 12th February. M & H.L. received secret instructions	
	11		Entrench from 11th to A.M. 15th. We proceeded	
	12		routine	
	13		routine	
	14		routine	
	15		routine	
	16		routine	
	17	3.0 p.m.	led lyth Typhoid Western in 3 trains for Embarkt at SOUTHAMPTON arrived SOUTHAMPTON and left 8 p.m. in S.S. MAIDAN. A draft 74 men joined	
	18	1.30 a.m.	4 lorries lyth Typhoid Expsh't Putrain for Embarkation in 8 trains, arrived SOUTH-AMPTON and left at 8 p.m. in S.S. N.W. MILLER	
HAVRE	19	11.0 a.	arrived HAVRE Finished dis Embarking 4.30 p.m. and went to Rest Camp Columns followed.	
	20		A Batt. H.Q. left at 4.20 a.m. B Batt. & C Batt. at 9.30 D Batt 12	
	21		A + H.Q. arrived at BERGUETTE 12.30 a.m. and marched WITTERNESS	

Army Form C. 2118

WAR DIARY
or
INTELLIGENCE SUMMARY
(Erase heading not required.)

Instructions regarding War Diaries and Intelligence Summaries are contained in F. S. Regs., Part II. and the Staff Manual respectively. Title Pages will be prepared in manuscript.

Place	Date	Hour	Summary of Events and Information	Remarks and references to Appendices
VITERNESS 22	23rd		In front when he called till the morning. Wet & fine. B.C. v D batteries arrived during day & the Column at night.	
	24th		Received 76 rounds H.E. per gun and 70 rounds shrapnel per gun from the Column. Our ammunition group is 400 rounds. I should have said that BERGUETTE station was bombed with 9 bombs from an aeroplane about 11 p.m. on the 25th. When the train A.13.15 should have got there & the train had not been hit. However very cold.	
	25th		Nothing very cold. Train arriving.	
			Bn MA mine exploded from 6 mines to MAZINGHEM . 2 miles west from here my 3rd Gun an order killed in front on west to MAZINGHEM very cold — winter	
	26th			
	27th		Marched up at 11.30 a.m. B Bde + H.Q. K ROMBLY (remember)	
	28th		Rennert when kept right at Foss FOMBLY was billeted in the morning B Battery H.Q + med in H.Q. at the Baron de Fransville Chateau or MAZINGHEM	
	29th		10.30 inspected R. & other units made by G.O.C. R.C.Flags. John M Kelly	

WAR DIARY
or
INTELLIGENCE SUMMARY

(Erase heading not required.)

182 / 2nd A.F.A.

Army Form C. 2118

Place	Date	Hour	Summary of Events and Information	Remarks and references to Appendices
MAZINGHEM	1.3.16		2 officers & No. 1, 6 layers and 6 elephants per battery went up to the Bde. & 12 gns.	
"	2.3.16		In 3 days instruction	
"	3.3.16		routine	
"	4.2.16		routine	
"	5.2.16		The party from the Front returned. The O.C., adjg officer, 2 officers per battery, 2 no. 1, 6 layers & 6 elephants per battery	
			were attached to a Group 12" D— provisionally	
"	6.3.16		routine	
"	7.3.16		routine	
			The party returned from the Front. The Brigade moved from MAZINGHEM to	
BELLERY	8.3.16		BELLERY, 6 miles south.	
"	9.3.16		The vehicles & gunners per battery went up to the Front the attached 4th 15" gns	
"	10.3.16		Routine	
"	11.3.16		Routine	
"	12.3.		The officers returned from Front	
"	13.3		The other sections of gunners went up to Front the 4th 15" D. bat.	
"	14.3		ink	
"	15.3		routine	
"	16.3		section return	
"	17.3		Any air worth march	

Army Form C. 2118

WAR DIARY
or
INTELLIGENCE SUMMARY
(Erase heading not required.)

Instructions regarding War Diaries and Intelligence Summaries are contained in F.S. Regs., Part II. and the Staff Manual respectively. Title Pages will be prepared in manuscript.

Place	Date	Hour	Summary of Events and Information	Remarks and references to Appendices
BELLERY	18/3/16		C.O. & telephonists from Bde Staff and 1 Section per Bty went up to front for week's attachment to 1st, 12th, & 15th Div. Bdes.	
-"-	19"		Routine.	
-"-	20"		-"-	
-"-	21"		23 Remounts arrived from Base.	
-"-	22"		Capt. Mr. Glendinning joined & assumed command of 'B' Battery.	
-"-	23"		Draft of 3 artificers joined & were posted to batteries. 5 Gunners joined from Base.	
-"-	24"		Lt. Col. H.F. Askwith joined & assumed command of Brigade.	
-"-	25"		Lt. Col. H.F. Askwith proceeded on leave to England. Gnr R.N. Bale left Bde. on account of illness.	
-"-	26"	12.30p	Lt. Col. A.G. Short left for England. Sections changed for training with 1st, 12th & 15th Div Bdes.	
-"-	27"		Routine	
-"-	28"		-"-	
-"-	29"		-"-	
-"-	30"		-"-	
-"-	31"		Lt. H.F. Askwith rejoined. Routine.	

H.T. Colquhoun Capt.
D. a. Adjt.
R.F.A.
1st Bde. R.F.A.

WAR DIARY or INTELLIGENCE SUMMARY

Army Form C. 2118

182nd BDE R.F.A. Vol 3

XVI

Place	Date	Hour	Summary of Events and Information	Remarks and references to Appendices
BELLERY	1/4/16	-	Received detailed instructions for training of B/182 as a counter-battery from 3rd to 20th April. Routine work.	M.D
"	2/4/16	-	Owing to sections being attached to 1st 12" + 15" Div. Art. for training, section opts at Bellike only able to attend to horses + carry out gun drill, rifle drill &c. Fine weather + making horse + better. Horse lines have been very bad. Routine.	M.D
"	3/4/16	-	" "	M.D
"	4/4/16	-	General machine work. Lt Capt M.F. Calvert who this day attached to 48 F.A. T.A.T. Wahrenf took over duties of Capt Fox Bell on his staff	M.D
"	5/4/16	-	20 men posted to us from B/182. Today we received cleared instructions from H.Qrs R. Arty 16 DIV route march. Col Askwith, C.M.G is I/c the C.R.A. 2nd Lt A.T. MacDuff acting Bde Major S/N C/182 posted acting Staff Capt	M.D
"	6/4/16	-	Routine.	M.D
"	7/4/16	-	We moved today on an Route Reach in conjunction with 15 Div.	M.D
Eshee Blaaren	8/4/16	-	Batteries carried out getting in and out of action quickly, general Bty work.	M.D
"	9/4/16	-	Return from Div training today inspected on Route by G.O.C 15th Div.	M.D
Bellery	10/4/16	-	Major Steel rejoined and took command B/182. Capt Bell struck off strength of Bde. Cert. A.a. 2nd/6.10.00 dates 5/4/16 W/S	M.D
"	11/4/16	-	Amplified Sections of A+D Btys took over positions of A/72 and D/72 15 DIV R.A. as R/c line. Relief 7/5/16	" "
"	12/4/16	-	Relieved section C/180 on line. Sections of B+D Btys took over position of A/72+B/72 15 DIV R.A. Sec of C/182 relieved section C/180 on line.	M.D
"	13/4/16	-	General Routine. Col H.F. Askwith C.M.G. proceeded to leave to take over H.Q.	M.D
"	14/4/16	-	Routine	M.D
"	15/4/16	-	do	M.D
"	16/4/16	-	B.H.Q. and H.Q. 182nd Bde proceeded to post today Kemper controlling relief with R. 15 DIV	M.D

WAR DIARY or INTELLIGENCE SUMMARY

Army Form C. 2118

Place	Date	Hour	Summary of Events and Information	Remarks and references to Appendices
VERMELLES	17/4/16		Registering	W.D
"	18/4/16		do	W.D
"	19/4/16		do	
"	20/4/16		No shooting	W.D
"	21/4/16		Retaliation for Trench Mortars	
"	22/4/16		Registration and retaliation	
"	23/4/16		Some retaliation	
"	24/4/16		do	W.D
"	25/4/16		do and heavy shelling m and opposite craters	W.D
"	26/4/16		All quiet in front.	W.D
"	27/4/16	5 a.m.	GAS ATTACK. All guns open fire immediately. Heavy shelling of Btys and Hd [?] and H.E. shells	W.D
"	"	5.45.	Gas reached Btys and all communications between H.Qs and Btos cut, not excepted of D/182 and C Bty who we got thro' D/182, also D/182 in Communic cables not O.P wire. Report heavy shelling of support lines	W.D
"	"	6.0	Message from 49th Infantry Bde. "S.O.S." GAS, sent to C.S. runners tried to get to A.B, they rung to GAS, and heavy shelling could not reach Btys.	W.D
"	"	6.20 a.m	Two runners try to get to H.Q Btys to ascertain position on their front, but unable to [?]	W.D
"	"	7.0	hostile shelling and GAS, cannot reach the Btys.	W.D
"	"	8.0	Btys still firing, no definite information to hand, all wires to C/D/182 cut by shelling	W.D
"	"		All no definite news	W.D

WAR DIARY
or
INTELLIGENCE SUMMARY

(Erase heading not required.)

Army Form C. 2118

Place	Date	Hour	Summary of Events and Information	Remarks and references to Appendices
VERMELLES	27/7/16	8.15	Gas lifted. Heavy rate of fire still kept up under orders from D.A.H.Q.	
"	"	9.0.	Everything reported quiet from A/182. Fire ceased for a short period until orders to continue by D.A.H.Q.	
"	"	10.10	D.A.H.Q. orders A/182 to quicken up rate to 3 p[er] jn[?] 5 sec	
"	"	10.25	Orders to slacken rate of fire 7 secs (by D.A.H.Q.) (B[rig?] Gen Rosso orders) passed to Sta[tions]	
"	"	10.40	Telephonic communication with A Bty for first time since attack started. Bty report all quiet.	
"	"	10.55	All Btys now report all quiet.	
"	"	11.0	A/182 ordered to increase rate of fire to 10 secs. B.H.Q. orders 3 p[er] jn[?]	
"	"	11.20	Reduce rate of fire. Big fire 1 minute, warning given to Btys to expect gas attack from Hulluch.	
"	"	11.30	Message from Infantry states :- No enemy in any part of my front line. D.A.H.Q. orders us to stop fire but keep sharp lookout. all quiet.	
"	"	8.0 p.	Gas alarm. Quiet opened immediately, but it proved false alarm. Registering	
"	28th	"		
"	29th	4 am	S.O.S. Gas received from G/actg[?]. Guns opened fire immediately but as soon as	

WAR DIARY or INTELLIGENCE SUMMARY

Army Form C. 2118

(Erase heading not required.)

Instructions regarding War Diaries and Intelligence Summaries are contained in F.S. Regs., Part II. and the Staff Manual respectively. Title Pages will be prepared in manuscript.

Place	Date	Hour	Summary of Events and Information	Remarks and references to Appendices
VERMELLES	29/4/16	4.30 am	Guns still firing, but no gas reached Bys, only from Lachrymatory shells.	WD
"	"	5.30 am	F.O.O. reports all quiet on front. Guns stood firing and Bys stand to.	WD
"	"	8.0 am	Gas alarm from Infantry, precautionary.	WD
"	"	9.0 am	All quiet. Registering.	WD
"	30/4/16	"	do	WD
"	"	10 am	Group System came in force. Col. H.F. Askwith C.M.G. being in command of left Group, which consists of 182nd Bde.F.A. and 177 Bde. B/77 Bde. and reinforcing Bty of Howitzers B/65 Bde.	WD

1875 Wt. W593/826 1,000,000 4/15 J.B.C. & A. A.D.S.S./Forms/C. 2118.

182 R.F.A. Vol 4

Confidential (16)

War diary of 182nd Bde R.F.A.
from 1st May 1916 to 31st May 1916

Army Form C. 2118

182nd Brigade R.F.A. from 1st May to 31st May 1916

WAR DIARY
or
INTELLIGENCE SUMMARY
(Erase heading not required.)

Instructions regarding War Diaries and Intelligence Summaries are contained in F. S. Regs., Part II. and the Staff Manual respectively. Title Pages will be prepared in manuscript.

Place	Date	Hour	Summary of Events and Information	Remarks and references to Appendices
VERMELLES	1/5/16	—	Normal. General Routine	M.S.
"	2/5/16	7.45pm	"GAS ATTACK" received from INFANTRY, proved to be false. Guns opened immediately. Normal Registration and usual retaliation	M.S.
"	3/5/16	1.30am	S.O.S. GAS Given by 44th INF. again proved to be false. All Guns opened barrage. Registration and usual retaliation. Enemy machine gun firing on our aeroplanes were silenced by B/By 182nd	M.S.
"	4/5/16	1.20am	False GAS attack. Guns opened barrage.	M.S.
"	"	1.30am	All quiet.	
"	"	10am	Registration and retaliation	
"	"	2.30pm	Hostile T. Mortars silenced	
"	"	6.15pm	Dispersed Hostile Infantry leaving Trench	
"	5/5/16	—	Retaliation, and dispersing working parties. Also registering suspicion at H.nub.26	M.S.
"	6/5/16	—	Normal General Routine.	M.S.
"	7/5/16	—	do do.	M.S.
"	8/5/16	—	Retaliation for hostile fire only	M.S.
"	9/5/16	12noon	Fired on suspected machine gun emplacement under construction. 5 direct hits by A.182.	M.S.
"	10/5/16	—	Registration and usual retaliation	M.S.
"	11/5/16	morning	Normal.	M.S.
"	"	4.10pm	Enemy started to barrage our suspicions with every description of shell, including	

WAR DIARY or INTELLIGENCE SUMMARY

Army Form C. 2118

182nd Brigade R.F.A.

from May 1st to May 31st 1916

(Erase heading not required.)

Place	Date	Hour	Summary of Events and Information	Remarks and references to Appendices
VERMELLES	11/5/16	4.15	Gas Shell. All Btys stood to on enemy trenches, but few retals. Answered on own front	MLS
"	"	4.30	Enemy shell shelling VERMELLES heavily	MLS
"	"	6.0	No abatement of bombardment	MLS
"	"	6.15	Shelling easing	MLS
"	"	6.30	Shelling ceased, everything normal.	MLS
"	12/5/16	—	Retaliation for Trench Mortars and rifle grenades working party dispersed.	MLS
"	13/5/16	—	Routine. All instructions re flooding trench issued by N.A.F.A.	MLS
"	14/5/16	—	do	MLS
"	15/5/16	—	Retaliation and usual registration. Dispersed working party	MLS
"	16/5/16	—	A.C.D Bty 182d prepare to take over new positions. Guns being handed over to NAFA	MLS
"	17/5/16	—	Normal. B. Bty withdrew to wagon lines	MLS
LOOS	18/5/16	—	H.Q. Rgt Group moved to Re Qrs B/s. Relieving RIGHT GROUP under Col. MR ASKWITH. C/182 B/180 and 477 join us. ORS 177 moves to LEFT GROUP. A Section of B/182 joined A/80 and a section to B/180. B/182 is still up and Sections sent to B/82 and B/82. A/B/C/D armament 6 gun Btys Lite wise B/B/B/B.	MLS
"	19/5/16	—	Registration with Btys	MLS
"	20/5/16	—	Registration & retaliation	MLS
"	21/5/16	—	Registration.	MLS
"	22/5/16	—	Registration of zones of BIV on own right in case of attack. Also registration with new correction for bar	MLS

WAR DIARY
or
INTELLIGENCE SUMMARY

Army Form C. 2118

182nd Bde R.F.A. from May 1st to May 31st 1916

(Erase heading not required.)

Instructions regarding War Diaries and Intelligence Summaries are contained in F. S. Regs., Part II. and the Staff Manual respectively. Title Pages will be prepared in manuscript.

Place	Date	Hour	Summary of Events and Information	Remarks and references to Appendices
LOOS	23/5/16	cont.d	and Range Shoot	WD
"		10.35	Registration for wire cutting	WD
"		noon	Retaliation.	WD
"	24/5/16	aft. shy.	Retaliation for hostile shelling of Loos.	WD
"	25/5/16	"	Registrations for concentrations of fire, for purposes of retaliation	WD
"	26/5/16		Routine	WD
"	27/5/16		Registration for barrage scheme, and retaliation.	WD
"	28/5/16	5.0	Retaliation for very heavy enemy shelling	WD
"	29/5/16	9am	D/162 registered by means of aeroplane. Working parties divisions	WD
"	30/5/16	7.30am	Retaliation for T.M.s, and rifle grenades.	WD
"			Normal.	WD

H. F. Cokworth
Col R.A.
O.C. 182 Bde R.F.A.

182 R.F.A
Vol 5
June

Confidential

War diary of
182nd Bde R. F. A.
from
1st June to 30th June 1916

182nd Bde R.F.A.

Army Form C. 2118

WAR DIARY
or
INTELLIGENCE SUMMARY
(Erase heading not required.)

Instructions regarding War Diaries and Intelligence Summaries are contained in F.S. Regs, Part II. and the Staff Manual respectively. Title Pages will be prepared in manuscript.

Place	Date	Hour	Summary of Events and Information	Remarks and references to Appendices
LOOS-SOUENT	1/6/16	—	Registration, working parties fired on. Normal day	Officers
do	2/6/16	—	Normal. Routine	Officers
do	3/6/16	11 a.m.	HQ's Right Group moved from Le Brebis to Mazingarbe Avenue. at 2.30.p.m. B.to registered and usual retaliation for enemy mortars and hostile fire. Some quiet on front.	Officers
do	4/6/16	—	General Routine.	Officers
"	"	4.30.	Successful firing by aeroplane done by C.B. of 77 Bde. (R Group)	Officers
do	5/6/16	—	Registration and retaliation for hostile shelling. Working parties fired on and dispersed.	Officers
do	6/6/16	—	Registration and retaliation. Normal day.	Officers
do	7/6/16	—	Working parties fired on and dispersed	Officers
do	8/6/16	—	Retaliation for T. Mortars	Officers
do	9/6/16	—	B.77 registration by aeroplane, aeroplane observer reports good shooting. Normal.	Officers
do	10/6/16	3.40 A.m.	B.77. retaliation for enemy bombing, W04 Runfl parties fired on during day	Officers
do	11/6/16	6.25/16 8.20pm	B.80 registered by aeroplane. 4 Targets engaged. Retaliation.	Officers

1875 Wt. W 593/826 1,000,000 4/15 J.B.C. & A. A.D.S.S./Forms/C.2118.

WAR DIARY or INTELLIGENCE SUMMARY

182nd Bde R.F.A.

Army Form C. 2118

Place	Date	Hour	Summary of Events and Information	Remarks and references to Appendices
LOOS SALIENT.	12/6/16	—	Retaliation. Registration on suspected T.M. emplacements by D.182.	Offr
do	13/6/16	—	Special registration of Point C. This point is a post selected for retaliation when called upon by the Infantry and is fired on by following Btys. D180, D180, C182, D180. map shooting M.B. 93 ±. Points A & B have also been selected for retaliation. A fired on by C182 D182 97 map. Shooting M.B.N. 2 ± ± ± B fired on by B77, D182, C182.	Offr
do	14/6/16	—	Retaliation "C". All Btys registered new sight lines due to D182 evacuating its position, and Zones altering slightly. 3 bdy HQ & OP returned to D180 for instructions.	Offr
do	15/6/16	—	Retaliation "A". Working parties fired on and driven in & emplacement examined.	Offr
do	16/6/16	—	Very quiet day. Registration.	Offr
do	17/6/16	—	Registration, working parties fired on, normal day	Offr
do	18/6/16	—	Suspected M.G. emplacement fired on, general routine	Offr
do	19/6/16	—	Routine	M.O.
do	20/6/16	—	Working parties fired on. Retaliation Point B, hostile O.P. engaged.	Offr
do	21/6/16	6-30pm	Retaliation point "D" for T. Mortar.	Offr
do	22/6/16	—	Reinforcement T. effect. Very quiet on front.	Offr

WAR DIARY or INTELLIGENCE SUMMARY

Army Form C. 2118

182nd Bde R.F.A

Place	Date	Hour	Summary of Events and Information	Remarks and references to Appendices
LOOS SALIENT	23/6/16	—	Registration Jap heads, wire & early front with good effect.	
do	24/6/16	1.4 pm	Retaliation Point A. ⎫ Retaliation forwarded shelling	
		4.30 "	do do A. ⎬	
		8.5 "	do do A.	
		9.20 "	do do A. ⎭	
do	25/6/16	12pm-3pm	B182 fired on enemy wire, made by Trench Mortars. During the day Bty carried out a systematic bombardment O.P.'s, Registration of "Soft Spots", Cross-Roads H.Qs M.G. emplacements & wire etc. Billets and communication also reported.	
do	26/6/16	—	Continued bombardment of enemy O.P.s and "Soft Spots" by Bty. Successful shooting reported by Bty.	
do	27/6/16	12.15AM	All Btys opened fire on enemy front line for 3 minutes. Rapid fire 10 secs (18pdrs) S.F. 20 Secs 4.5 Hows	
"	"	12.18am	Barrage lifted to enemy support line and kept barrage formed, 18pdr firing at Sec fire 15 sec, 4.5 Hows 30 secs	
"	"	12.30am	Firing continued	
"	"	1am	Firing still continued, raiding parties expected to return now, all firing to cease when blue rockets are sent up.	
"	"	2am	Still no news of raiding parties and Btys still firing at sec fire 15 secs, How S.F. 20 sec.	
"	"	3.30	Informed by Infantry raiders now returned, having successfully carried out programme.	

WAR DIARY
or
INTELLIGENCE SUMMARY

Army Form C. 2118

182nd Bde R.F.A.

Place	Date	Hour	Summary of Events and Information	Remarks and references to Appendices
LOOS SALIENT	27th	3.30 a.m.	Order sent to Btys to cease firing.	[signature]
		3.45		
do	28th	—	Infantry report on last night's raid reads — "Artillery fire which was most effective materially attributed to the success of the enterprise. Valuable assistance was also rendered by some Guns 1st Div. The enemy retaliated with 77mm and hy 2 and with Trench mortars on our trenches behind craters and on the "enclosure".	[signature]
do	28th	—	All quiet. Regs Posten. Working parties fired on.	
do	29th	1.0 am to 1.20 am	All 18 rdo Right Group fire on front line trenches at rate of 1 ty fire 10 secs	[signature]
"		1.20 to 1.40	B/82, C/77, B/182. Fire having lifted 200 yds and barrage at 10 secs Bty Fire A/180, B/180	
"		1.40 to 2.10	A + B/180 continue barrage, until informed by Inf. operations are over	
"		—	Btys continue to fire on billets, tracks, and communications	
"	30th	—	Btys again fired on suspected H.Qs tracks and communications	[signature]
"	30th	9.10	A/180, B/180, C/182, C/77, opened fire on enemy front line for 3 mins with H.E. Fire lifted 200 x and rate of fire reduced to B.F. 20 secs for 5 mins, ½ B.E. 5 mins	
		9.17		
"	30th	9.22	Fire ceases. B/182, A/182, A/180 are lent to 1st Div for the night	

W A R   D I A R Y

182nd Brigade
Royal Field Artillery

1st. July to 31st. July 1916.

VOLUME NO. 6̶ 7.

broken up 27.8.16.

16 July
182 R.F.A
Vol 6

WAR DIARY
or
INTELLIGENCE SUMMARY
(Erase heading not required.)

Army Form C. 2118

Instructions regarding War Diaries and Intelligence Summaries are contained in F. S. Regs, Part II. and the Staff Manual respectively. Title Pages will be prepared in manuscript.

Place	Date	Hour	Summary of Events and Information	Remarks and references to Appendices
LOOS SALIENT	1/7/16	12 AM to 12 p.m.	Enemy retaliatory batteries active, shelling our front line and support trenches at intervals during the day. Retaliation on Groups "A" & "D" front.	R.W.S
do	2/7/16	—	Situation quiet, normal work was carried on.	R.W.S
do		10.56 to 10 pm	B/180, B/182, C/182 arranged with Infantry shrapnel fire at 85 roses on enemy lines. Re Infantry shelling was on smoke. The enemy retaliated fired on along front.	R.W.S
		10.30 – 10.38	Above Bties opened 15½ minutes on enemy lines. The enemy retaliation was very slight. Bties stand for again for 2 mins doing shrapnel. 15 midnight all quiet again.	
		11.35 – 11.37		
do	3/7/16	—	Suspected O.P's. T.M. emplacements & T.M.G. machinegun emplacements were effectually dealt with throughout the day. Air report a number of slow hits on our wire & a long burst of fire visible.	R.W.S
do	4/7/16	—	Slightly increased hostile fire on our front & support trenches at intervals from squares "A", "B" & "D".	R.W.S
do	5/7/16	—	Situation normal. 3e retaliated on enemy's G.P.'s on enemy line. Becoming rather bad.	R.W.S
do	6/7/16	—	Situation normal. Retaliation carried out for hostile shelling of front & support lines. Our T.M's were active, with good results. Also on Re Left & Left Group fire a number of shots.	R.W.S

Army Form C. 2118

WAR DIARY
or
INTELLIGENCE SUMMARY
(Erase heading not required.)

Instructions regarding War Diaries and Intelligence Summaries are contained in F. S. Regs., Part II. and the Staff Manual respectively. Title Pages will be prepared in manuscript.

Place	Date	Hour	Summary of Events and Information	Remarks and references to Appendices
LOOS SALIENT	7/7/16	—	Enemy arty more active today than usual. LOOS was shelled at intervals. EKWAR MAZINGARBE. We retaliated during the day on hostile pos'n our hows. ty. good line. Our T.Ms engaged in cutting wire at M5.c.2.5½, M5.a.1 wire in front of Albian gptcwurd M5.C.5. M16c.9.8 + M6.39.5½. with good effect.	Allus
do	8/7/16	—	Enemy again rather active. LOOS was shelled. During the morning with 4.2". 5.9" engaged Hostile T.Ms. Working parties were and retaliation carried out. T.Ms continue to cut wire at M5.C.3.5½.	Allus
do	9/7/16	—	Enemy much quieter today. MAZINGARBE was shelled, as retaliated by shooting on ARE ST LAURENT. T.Ms again cutting wire M5.C.2.5½. Abnormal No of hostile shellows exs	Allus
do	10/7/16	—	Very quiet day. Registration carried out, our T.Ms engaged enemy more effectively as he points selected M.S. C.2.5.5. + M5.d.8.5¾ + M5.d.y?.4½.	Allus
do	11/7/16	—	Very little enemy activity today, working parties fired on effectively. Harassment not aeroplane giving G.F Targets. Our T.Ms again did very good work, on wire as before as before	Allus
do	12/7/16	—	Enemy rather active, shelling LOOS, + MAROC rather heavily. Our retaliation retaliation. Our T.Ms continued to cut wire	Allus
do	13/7/16	—	Very quiet day.	Allus

Army Form C. 2118

WAR DIARY or INTELLIGENCE SUMMARY
(Erase heading not required.)

Place	Date	Hour	Summary of Events and Information	Remarks and references to Appendices
LOOS SALIENT	14/7/16	—	Fairly quiet day. Pips/Seanbs were fired into LOOS, & enemy T.M's were rather active on Trenches between Harrisons Craters and Double Crassier. Our T.M.'s retaliated with good effect. T.M's continued wire cutting.	[sig]
do	15/7/16	—	Fosse 7 was rather heavily shelled this morning with 5.9's from direction of PT 75 ST EDOURD. Btys carried out a shot with R.F.C. on GF targets. Retaliation given during day. Observation & conditions not good.	[sig]
"	"	11/5 pm	As arranged a mine was blown near Seaforth Crater. At 11.25 pm the following Btys opened a barrage round Seaforth Crater. The following Btys being engaged B/82. C/77. C/182 A/180. B/90 These Btys 18 pdrs opened fire at B.F. 10 secs. 2 Btys of the 40th Div went West B/88 & B/81. The How's D/82 & D/180 opened fire on selected points at RF 20 secs. The 60 pdrs were also used.	[sig]
"	"	11.20 pm	Btys ceased firing	[sig]
"	"	11.45	Owing to hostile fire we retaliated near Harrisons Crater, Point A.	
"	"	11.50	Retaliate "A" again given owing to hostile fire.	
"	16/7/16	12.35 am	Enemy opened fire on & around SEAFORTH CRATER, we retaliated.	[sig]
"	16/7/16	12.45 am	At request of Infantry, C/77. C/182. B/180 & B/182 reopened original barrage, owing to heavy shelling & machine gun fire around SEAFORTH CRATER.	[sig]
"	"	12.55	Infantry report all quiet.	

WAR DIARY
or
INTELLIGENCE SUMMARY
(Erase heading not required.)

Army Form C. 2118

Instructions regarding War Diaries and Intelligence Summaries are contained in F. S. Regs., Part II. and the Staff Manual respectively. Title Pages will be prepared in manuscript.

Place	Date	Hour	Summary of Events and Information	Remarks and references to Appendices
LOOS SALIENT	16/7/16	7.15 pm	An aeroplane fell on enemy terrain opposite LUMBERON ALLEY, about H.31.D.2.55.	[signature]
do	do	2.0 pm	All guns again	[signature]
do	do	—	Fairly Quiet day, Loos lightly shelled with bjb ourindo during afternoon the enemy bombarded trenches between HARTS & HARRISON'S CRATERS, with bjb grenades and tp.2.s we retaliated.	[signature]
do	17/7/16	—	Very Quiet day, Little shelling on either side, observation conditions not good owing to low visibility.	[signature]
do	18/7/16	—	Hostile artillery fairly active today, our trenches at various points being shelled we retaliated. MAZINGARBE was also shelled during the afternoon. H.31.D.6.Mo bombarded selected point at H.31.D.1.3. for 3 men at B.F.5.ses. This was at request of Infantry owing to machine guns interfering with construction of top of Seaforth Crater.	[signature]
do	19/9/16	—	Enemy Artillery fairly active again today to which we replied. Hostile T.M's. shelled behind HART'S CRATER during afternoon.	[signature]
do	20/7/16	—	Normal day. Slight hostile fire to which we replied. Our T.Ms fired with good effect near HARTS & HARRISONS CRATERS.	[signature]
do	21/7/16	—	Normal day. Retaliation carried out several new retaliation points allotted	[signature]

Army Form C. 2118

WAR DIARY
or
INTELLIGENCE SUMMARY
(Erase heading not required.)

Instructions regarding War Diaries and Intelligence Summaries are contained in F.S. Regs., Part II. and the Staff Manual respectively. Title Pages will be prepared in manuscript.

Place	Date	Hour	Summary of Events and Information	Remarks and references to Appendices
LOOS SALIENT	21/7/16	—	Inf. Infantry wire registered. Other as usual today. Front at present held by R Group 15th Div Arty. Reliefs to take place on 22/23rd and 23/24th.	Allies
do	22/7/16	10.30 A.m.	Very quiet day initial. Bty withdrawn to take over 15th DIV positions. Section only A/73, B/82 relieve A/72, B/72. C/182 relieve our present position. C/182 relieve A/73. B/82 relieve D/72. D/72 & D/73 relieve C/72 & D/72 & D/73 and D/79 over from this group.	Allies
	23rd	2.0 p.m	relieve B/72 & B/79 relief A/70 and D/79 over from this group.	
		3.0 p.m	First night of relief complete.	Allies
		10.0 p.m	Very quiet day. Our trenches slightly shelled. No casualties. Bty Group lines moved one section. Positions A/182 L36.6.0. B/182 F25d.0.5 C/182 F26d.2.1. D/182 . Bty left and Ammunition Dump . New H.Q. at G.13.d.2.35.	Allies
HULLUCH SECTOR	24th	2 am	Relief of 15th DA complete.	
"	25th	—	Registration of new front which now extends from 41.9.a.92.35 to G.12.a.3.35 carried out. Little hostile activity, one form on T.M. HQ wagon line moved to L.2.6.63.9.	Allies
"	25th	—	Enemy rather active during afternoon. Vermelles being shelling with 5.9" during afternoon. Counter-registration carried out. Our T.M. active to which enemy replied.	Allies
"	26th	—	Fairly quiet day again, everything parties engaged. Nothing to report.	Allies
"	27th	—	Normal day. Nothing to report.	Allies

Army Form C. 2118

WAR DIARY
or
INTELLIGENCE SUMMARY
(Erase heading not required.)

Instructions regarding War Diaries and Intelligence Summaries are contained in F. S. Regs., Part II. and the Staff Manual respectively. Title Pages will be prepared in manuscript.

Place	Date	Hour	Summary of Events and Information	Remarks and references to Appendices
HULLUCH SECTOR	28/7/16	—	Retaliations carried out & registrations. Enemy artillery rather more active than yesterday.	J.West
"	29/7/16	—	A 77cc Sun at bungles fired on our Trenches in G12a & G6bd. The retaliation Enemy T.M.s active. Registration by aeroplane carried out by D.77.	J.West
"	30/7/16	—	A very quiet day. Heavy T.M.s were rather active. A heavy T.M. emplacement suspected at H.13.a.3.7. was fired on effectively.	J.West
"	31/7/16	—	Very quiet day. We carried out retaliations & registered suspected H.Q. at G.7.a.6.2a.9." and T.M. emplacement at G.12.a.6.7.1/2. Enemy blew a small mine at G.12.c.5.1/2.8.3/4 doing damage to our Sap.	J.West

H.J. Ashworth Lt Col
O.C. 182 ~B~ R.F.A.

www.ingramcontent.com/pod-product-compliance
Lightning Source LLC
Chambersburg PA
CBHW081504160426
43193CB00014B/2585